D.W.
(Don't Worry)

Judy M. Hill
with illustrations by
Jennifer D. Sain

© Judy Hill 2011

All rights reserved. No part of this book may be
reproduced or transmitted in any form or by any means,
electronic or mechanical or by any information or storage
and retrieval system without permission
in writing from the author or publisher.

Published by AKA:yola / AKA-Publishing
Columbia, Missouri
www.akayola.com
www.aka-publishing.com

Illustrated by Jennifer D. Sain

ISBN: 978-1-936688-15-9

Preface

The day my mother was born, her mom died. As an infant she was taken to the home of her grandmother who had already raised nine children and now had another little baby to care for. At age twelve, my mother's grandmother died. Mom asked Aunt Hilda if she could live with her and her two children who were cousins.

Worry was a part of my mom's life. As a nurse, I see worry in the eyes of patients, friends and others. Putting my hand on their upper right chest, I tell them, "This is where you turn off the 'worry button'—I am now turning it off." Smiles come to their face and shoulders drop three inches as the "Don't Worry" takes effect.

I refuse to worry. I know God will take care of me; He will give me plenty of food, water and clothing to wear. He is always with me and will always be my Provider. I am precious to Him and will not go without things I need.

Don't Worry! —Judy Hill

"If your worry button is turned on, please turn it off or have someone turn it off for you. It is located above your heart near your shoulder."
—Judy Hill

Attracted by the litter of wiry haired puppies twirling, nibbling, and playing with each other, a crowd of people gathered near the pickup in the parking lot:

1

FREE PUPPIES!

Curious, I sauntered over to take a peek. One little pup caught my eye. He was curled up from his nose to his tail in a straw-tufted corner in the bed of the red pickup.

He looked round, brownish red and worried as I reached out to pet him.

"You need this one," began one of the twin boys in his most salesmanship manner. He pointed to the worried little puppy in the corner. "Look," he continued as he picked up the puppy, "he has short hair." He did look different than the others.

While the other puppies danced around the bed of the pickup, this one lay by himself. He peered up at me sadly with a bashful, yet expressive and hopeful glance.

"Nope," I said. I was not going to let myself be interested. "Not for me," I thought as I started away into the parking lot to do my Saturday shopping.

My mind was made up. I didn't need a puppy. I left the "Free Puppies," got my shopping cart, and started toward the items on my list. I pushed the cart past the cereal, bread, milk, iced cookies, apples, chicken and potatoes, and even the school supplies.

My shopping list was being ignored. I found my cart filling up, but not with groceries and school supplies! Instead I was getting a soft bed, a bag of food, treats, water bowl, collar, leash, and red bandana.

I pushed the cart faster and faster to the check out, paid for the pet supplies and flew into the parking lot as fast as I could go.

"Is he still here?" I called out.

By this time, I was praying that the shy puppy was still curled up in the pickup, waiting for me. Please, oh please! But, no! The worried little face wasn't there to greet me.

I was sad. I had a heart, a place for him. I was already picturing the children on my block playing with him. Slowly I turned away to return the bed, the collar, doggy bowl...

One of the twin boys called, smiling, "I have been holding him for you until you got back." I turned around and there he was in the same curled position, now in the arms of the boy with outstretched hands.

Pulling the puppy to me, the worried little creature settled into my arms. Happily, I carried him to the car and laid him on the floor of the car. He stayed.
"Don't worry," I told him as he rode home with me.
"Don't worry."

DW, I thought. That's his name—DW!
We were home before I had time to worry
about having a new member of the family.

As I tied the new red bandana around his neck, he looked up at me adoringly. He kept his gaze on me as we took our first walk together, with me smiling and DW's tail wagging the whole way. I wasn't worried the least little bit. I knew DW and I were going to be buddies forever.

"Therefore, I say to you, do not worry about your life, what you will eat or what you will drink, nor about your body; what you will put on. Is not life more than food and the body more than clothing?"   Matthew 6:25.NKJV

Meet the Author

Judith M. Kahler Hill lives in Columbia, Missouri with her husband Jim, who relishes her dedication and enthusiasm for family and life. She was born on her father's birthday in Keytesville, Missouri. She attended college with her three daughters and is a registered nurse.

Throughout her life as daughter, mother and nurse, she believes the miracle and acceptance of not worrying to be a fruit of her life and a natural gift that she loves to share with others. Watching others sitting in the rocking chair of worry that goes nowhere, she and DW gave birth to this first in a series of books, *D.W. (Don't Worry)*.

Meet the Illustrator

Jennifer D. George Sain lives with her family in Fulton, Missouri. She works as the Mildred M. Cox Gallery Director and the *Kemper Kids Create* Programing Coordinator at William Woods University where she is completing her B.A. in Art.

This project was done as an internship and part of her Senior Exit Show and portfolio. Jennifer has used a unique and imaginative medium, cut and torn paper. Children are asked to embrace the abstract, and apply their own imaginations to the simplicity of the images, thus making the work both educational and literary in scope.